ALL GOD'S CRITTERS GOT A PLACE IN THE CHOIR

ALL GOD'S CRITTERS GOT A PLACE IN THE CHOIR

words and music by
Bill Staines

pictures by Margot Zemach

A Puffin Unicorn

PUFFIN UNICORN BOOKS

Published by the Penguin Group
Penguin Books USA Inc., 375 Hudson Street, New York, New York 10014, U.S.A.
Penguin Books Ltd, 27 Wrights Lane, London W8 5TZ, England
Penguin Books Australia Ltd, Ringwood, Victoria, Australia
Penguin Books Canada Ltd, 10 Alcorn Avenue, Toronto, Ontario, Canada M4V 3B2
Penguin Books (N.Z.) Ltd, 182-190 Wairau Road, Auckland 10, New Zealand
Penguin Books Ltd, Registered Offices: Harmondsworth, Middlesex, England

Library of Congress number 88-31696
ISBN 0-14-054838-6

Published in the United States by Dutton Children's Books,
a division of Penguin Books USA Inc.
Designer: Riki Levinson
Printed in Hong Kong
First Puffin Unicorn Edition 1993
7 9 10 8 6

ALL GOD'S CRITTERS GOT A PLACE IN THE CHOIR is also available
in hardcover from Dutton Children's Books.

for Karen, Bowen, and Hallie

B.S.

for my sister, Amielle

M.Z.

All God's critters got a place in the choir—
Some sing low, some sing higher,
Some sing out loud on the telephone wire,

And some just clap their hands

Or paws

Or anything they got. Now . . .

Listen to the bass, it's the one on the bottom
Where the bullfrog croaks and the hippopotamus
Moans and groans with a big t'do,
    And the old cow just goes "Moo."

The dogs and the cats they take up the middle,

While the honeybee hums and the cricket fiddles.

The donkey brays and the pony neighs

And the old coyote howls.

All God's critters got a place in the choir—
Some sing low, some sing higher,
Some sing out loud on the telephone wire,
And some just clap their hands

    Or paws

        Or anything they got. Now . . .

Listen to the top where the little birds sing

On the melodies with the high notes ringing.

The hoot owl hollers over everything,

And the jaybird disagrees.

Singing in the nighttime, singing in the day,

The little duck quacks, then he's on his way.

The possum ain't got much to say,

    And the porcupine talks to himself.

All God's critters got a place in the choir—

Some sing low, some sing higher,

Some sing out loud on the telephone wire,

And some just clap their hands

    Or paws

        Or anything they got. Now . . .

It's a simple song of living sung everywhere
By the ox and the fox and the grizzly bear,

The grumpy alligator and the hawk above,
The sly raccoon and the turtledove.

All God's critters got a place in the choir—
Some sing low, some sing higher,
Some sing out loud on the telephone wire,

And some just clap their hands

Or paws

Or anything they got NOW!

CHORUS

All God's crit-ters got a place in the choir—Some sing low,

some sing high-er, Some sing out loud on the tel-e-phone wire, And

some just clap their hands Or paws Or an-y-thing they got. Now...

VERSE

Lis-ten to the bass, it's the one on the bot-tom Where the

bull-frog croaks and the hip-po-pot-a-mus Moans and groans with a

big— t'-do, And the old cow just goes "Moo."

VERSE

The dogs and the cats they take up the mid-dle, While the

hon-ey-bee hums and the crick-et fid-dles. The don-key brays and the

po—ny neighs And the old coy-o-te howls.

CHORUS

VERSE

Lis-ten to the top where the lit-tle birds sing On the

mel-o-dies with the high notes ring-ing. The hoot owl hol-lers o-ver

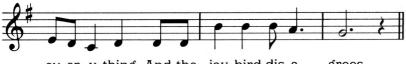

ev-er-y-thing, And the jay-bird dis-a - grees.

VERSE

Sing-ing in the night-time, sing-ing in the day, The

lit-tle duck quacks, then he's on his way.__ The pos-sum ain't got

much— to say, And the por-cu-pine talks to him-self.

CHORUS

VERSE

It's a sim-ple song of liv-ing sung ev-ery-where By the

ox and the fox and the griz-zly bear,— The grum-py al-li-ga-tor and the

hawk a-bove, The sly rac-coon— and the tur-tle-dove.

CHORUS

All God's crit-ters got a place in the choir—Some sing low,

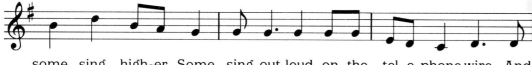

some sing high-er, Some sing out loud on the tel-e-phone wire, And

some just clap their hands Or paws Or an-y-thing they got NOW!